dabblelab

SOCK PUPPET THEATER PRESENTS

The Three Little Pigs

A Make and Play Production

by Christopher L. Harbo

CAPSTONE PRESS
a capstone imprint

Dabble Lab Books are published by Capstone Press,
1710 Roe Crest Drive, North Mankato, Minnesota 56003
www.mycapstone.com

Cataloging-in-Publication Data is available at the Library of Congress website.
ISBN: 978-1-5157-6683-4 (library binding)
ISBN: 978-1-5157-6687-2 (eBook PDF)

Editorial Credits

Juliette Peters, designer; Marcy Morin, puppet and prop creator;
Sarah Schuette, photo stylist; Morgan Walters, media researcher;
Tori Abraham, production specialist

Photo Credits

All photos by Capstone Studio, Karon Dubke with the exceptions of Shutterstock:
Aisyaqilumaranas, block 5, aniad, twigs 5, Lightspring, hay 5, linavita, bottom 28,
Mammut Vision, design element throughout, Pattern image, design element throughout,
photocell, design element throughout, Ruslan Kudrin, 21, Tsekhmister, 4, Vladitto, 26,
Yomka, design element throughout

Printed in Canada.
010395F17

About the Author

Christopher L. Harbo grew up watching *Sesame Street*, *Mister Rogers' Neighborhood*, and *The Muppet Show*. Ever since then, he's wanted to be a puppeteer — and now his dream has finally come true! In addition to puppetry, Christopher enjoys folding origami, reading comic books, and watching superhero movies.

Table of Contents

The Three Little Pigs

The tale of *The Three Little Pigs* has been told for centuries. But no one published it in a book until the 1800s. In fact, its most famous version appeared in *English Fairy Tales* by Joseph Jacobs in 1898. Since then the story has been retold in countless ways — sometimes with surprising twists.

Now you can put your own spin on *The Three Little Pigs*. The pages that follow provide clever ideas for creating and performing a complete sock puppet production. You'll find simple instructions for making the puppets, stage, and props. You'll also discover a full play script and helpful performance tips. So let's get started. An amazing make and play sock puppet show is at your fingertips!

The Plot

The classic story begins with three little pigs setting out on their own. All three build homes, but with materials of varying strength. The first pig chooses straw, the second uses sticks, and the third builds with bricks.

Soon, a wolf arrives at the straw house. When the pig refuses to let him in, the wolf blows down the house. In some stories, the wolf gobbles up the little pig. In others, the pig runs off to the second little pig's house.

Next, the wolf stops at the stick house. The second pig also refuses to open up, so the wolf blows down that house too. Once again, he gobbles the pig up in some tales. In others, the two pigs scamper off to the third pig's house.

Finally, the wolf arrives at the brick house. Locked out a third time, he tries to blow it down. But the sturdy home doesn't budge. Frustrated, the wolf climbs down the chimney and falls into a pot of boiling water. In some stories, the third pig cooks the wolf for dinner. In others, the wolf runs away, never to be seen again.

The Cast

Pigwaldo

Pigwaldo always looks for an easy solution to life's problems. It's no surprise that he picks the pile of straw to build his house. But he soon discovers that choosing the easy way out has its drawbacks.

Pigwena

Pigwena is slightly more practical than her brother, Pigwaldo. She knows a house of straw is a bad idea — but why carry bricks when sticks will do? She's confident her house will keep her snug and warm, no matter which way the wind blows.

Piggero

Piggero has his eyes on the future and is not afraid of a little hard work. He knows a house of bricks will be a chore to build — but it will also stand the test of time. When trouble comes knocking, it's Piggero's brains that save the three pigs' bacon!

Wolf

The wolf has one thing on his mind — HAM! He's hungry and will stop at nothing to sink his teeth into some pork chops. This villain is full of hot air — and he's not afraid to use it!

Sock Puppet Creation

Oh, my!
Let's scram!

Supplies to Create
The Three Pigs

- 3 large pink socks, in various shades
- 3 3.25-inch (8.3-cm) foam half balls
- cardboard
- pencil
- scissors
- craft glue
- dark pink felt
- light pink felt
- 6 googly eyes
- 3 pink buttons

1. Turn a sock inside out.

2. Place the flat side of the foam half ball on the cardboard. Trace around the base of the ball with a pencil.

3. Cut out the circle traced on the cardboard.

4. Fold the cardboard circle in half.

5. Glue one side of the folded cardboard to the base of the foam half ball. Line up the curve of the cardboard with the curved edge of the ball. The loose flap of cardboard will form the mouth of the puppet.

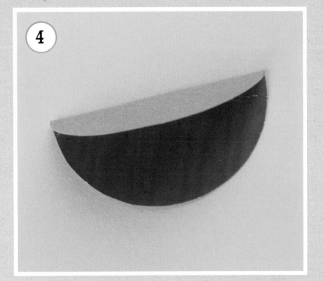

6. Apply glue to the inside of the top and bottom of the mouth. Tuck the toe of the sock into the mouth and allow the glue to dry.

7. Turn the sock right side out, pulling it over the foam half ball.

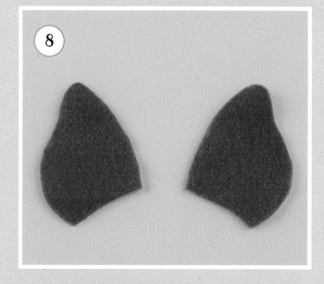

8. Cut two ear shapes out of the dark pink felt. Set aside.

9. Cut two smaller ear shapes out of the light pink felt. Glue the light pink inner ears to the dark pink outer ears.

10. Glue the completed ears to the puppet's head.

11. Glue googly eyes to the puppet's head.

12. Glue a button nose below the eyes to finish the first pig puppet.

13. Repeat steps 1 through 12 to complete the remaining two pig puppets.

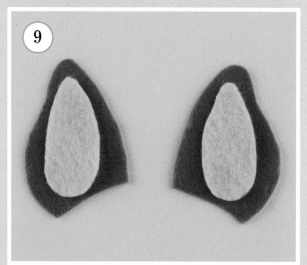

Who are
you calling mean
and nasty?!

Supplies to Create
Big Bad Wolf

- utility knife
- 2-inch (5-cm) foam egg
- cardboard
- pencil
- hot glue
- 3.25-inch (8.3-cm) foam half ball
- 2 1-inch (2.5-cm) foam balls
- large brown sock
- scissors
- white craft foam
- craft glue
- dark brown felt
- brown faux fur
- light brown felt
- googly eyes

1. With an adult's help, use a utility knife to cut the foam egg in half the long way.

2. Place the flat sides of the foam egg halves on the cardboard. Line them up so the wide ends are touching, back-to-back. Trace around the base of both egg halves with a pencil.

3. Cut out the cardboard egg shapes, but leave the two shapes connected where they meet.

4. Glue the cardboard egg shapes to the flat sides of the egg halves. Fold the egg halves toward each other until they meet to form one whole egg. The top half will serve as the upper jaw. The bottom half will serve as the lower jaw.

5. With an adult's help, hot glue the wide end of the upper jaw to the foam half ball. The flat side of the ball and the flat side of the upper jaw should line up. Once attached, the bottom jaw should be free to swing up and down.

6. Hot glue the two small foam balls side by side to the top of the foam half ball. This shape is the completed headpiece.

7. Slide the headpiece into the sock until the mouth stops at the end of the toe.

8. Pinch the sock's toe together between the upper and lower jaw. With an adult's help, hot glue the pinched fabric in place.

9. Cut out two pointy foam teeth. Glue them on either side of the mouth.

10. Cut a horseshoe-shaped mane out of the dark brown felt.

11. Glue the mane to the top and sides of the puppet's head.

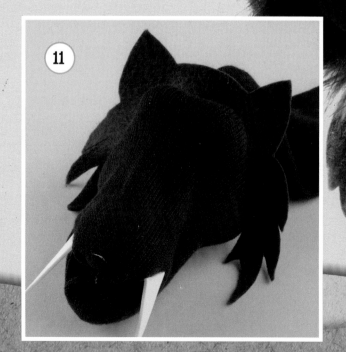

12. Glue googly eyes to the two bumps in the sock created by the foam balls on the headpiece.

13. Cut two ear shapes out of the faux fur. Set aside.

14. Cut two smaller ear shapes out of the light brown felt. Glue the light brown inner ears to the faux fur outer ears.

15. Glue the completed ears to the puppet's head.

16. Cut out a small patch of faux fur. Glue it below the mouth to give the finished wolf a hairy chest!

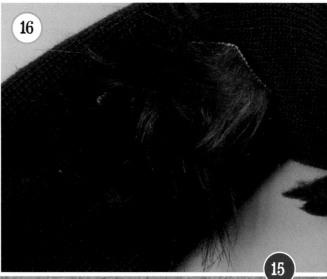

Stage and Prop Creation

Suggested Supplies:

- card table
- large blanket
- scissors
- yellow craft foam
- orange craft foam
- red craft foam
- craft glue
- straw
- twigs
- red felt
- black craft foam
- silver marker
- craft sticks
- tan craft foam

Stage:

1. Unfold two legs on a card table and use them to prop the table up on its side.

2. Drape a large blanket over the top of the card table. Try scrunching the blanket along the top edge of the table to make the stage look like a fancy curtain.

Houses:

1. Use a scissors to cut three house shapes out of yellow, orange, and red craft foam. Be sure to include a chimney on the red house.

2. Spread craft glue over the front of the yellow house. Sprinkle bits of straw on top of the glue to cover the front of the house completely. Let dry.

3. Spread craft glue over the front of the orange house. Lay twigs on top of the glue to cover the front of the house completely. Let dry.

4. Spread craft glue over the front of the red house. Cut small brick shapes out of red felt. Lay them in an organized pattern on the craft glue to cover the front of the house completely. Let dry.

5. Cut door and window shapes out of black craft foam. Use a silver marker to draw window panes and doorknobs on the shapes.

6. Glue the windows and doors to the front of each house any way you see fit.

7. Glue a craft stick to the bottom back side of each house to complete the props.

Piles of Materials:

1. Cut a small half circle out of tan craft foam. Spread craft glue over the front of the half circle. Cover the glue with bits of straw and let dry.

2. Glue a small pile of twigs together. Let dry.

3. Cut small brick shapes out of red felt. Glue them together in a small pile and let dry.

4. Glue the piles of straw, sticks, and bricks to the ends of craft sticks to complete the props.

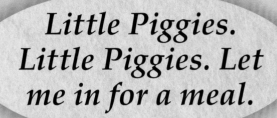

Now that the stage is set,
turn the page to read the script!

The Script

Narrator: Long ago, three little pigs named Piggero *(pops up)*, Pigwena *(pops up)*, and Pigwaldo *(pops up)* decided to move out on their own. As they walked together down the road, they kept their eyes peeled for materials to build their new homes. Before long, they came upon a welcome surprise . . . *(piles of materials pop up)*

Piggero: Ho, ho! Look at this. Someone has left piles of straw, sticks, and bricks just lying beside the road.

Pigwena: Who would do such a thing?

Pigwaldo: I don't know. But surely this is our lucky day. All three of us are in need of building materials for our homes.

Pigwena: Too true. Too true. With night fast approaching, a mean, nasty old wolf is sure to be prowling around.

Wolf: *(peeks up)* Hmph! Mean and nasty?! That's a bit harsh, don't you think?! *(ducks down)*

Piggero: *(reacting to wolf)* Riiiight . . . *(turning back to pigs)* Well, I'll gladly take the bricks. They're just what I need to build a strong and cozy home.

Pigwena: Go right ahead. There's no way I'm carrying those heavy bricks all over the countryside. I'll gladly take the sticks. A wooden house is strong enough for me — and not nearly as hard to build.

Pigwaldo: Are you both crazy?! Why bother with clunky sticks and heavy bricks? This light, fluffy straw will do just fine. What's more, I think I'll build my straw house right here!

Piggero: Suit yourselves! *(all three pigs and materials duck down)*

Narrator: And so, the three little pigs got to work building their homes. Pigwaldo did just want he said. In no time flat his straw house stood right beside the road.

Pigwaldo: *(straw house and pig pop up)* Ta-da! All done! Easy-peasy. *(both duck down)*

Narrator: Pigwena carried her sticks a short distance from the road. Her house took a little longer to build.

Pigwena: *(pushes stick house up with effort)* Whew! That was a lot of work. But I feel much safer in a stick house away from that busy road. *(both duck down)*

Narrator: Piggero lugged his bricks far from the road. His house took hours and hours to build.

Piggero: *(struggles to lift brick house)* UHH! OOF! GRUNT! There! It took forever, but this house — far from the road — will keep me safe and warm for years and years. *(both duck down)*

Narrator: Not long after the three little pigs snuggled into their homes, along came a mean, nasty, and very hungry wolf. *(wolf walks on stage)*

Wolf: *(looking around for narrator)* Who are you calling mean and nasty?

Narrator: Riiiight . . . Anyway, the first house he spied sat right beside the road. *(straw house pops up)*

Wolf: What have we here?! Do I smell a wee-little pig in that straw hut?

Pigwaldo: *(peeking out from behind house)* Uh-oh!

Wolf: Little piggy. Little piggy. Let me in for a meal.

Pigwaldo: *(peeking out from behind house, shaking)* No way, José! It's my life you'll steal!

Wolf: Who is José? No matter, prepare to feel my fury! *(huffs and puffs and blows the straw house offstage)*

Pigwaldo: *(stands shivering)* Oh, dear! Time to skedaddle! *(runs offstage)*

Wolf: *(chasing)* Oh, no you don't.

Narrator: The hungry wolf chased Pigwaldo all the way to the house of sticks. *(stick house pops up)*

Wolf: *(to audience)* What luck! That little porker led me straight to his sister's house! The menu just doubled in size!

Wolf: *(to house)* Little piggies. Little piggies. Let me in for a meal.

Pigwena: *(both pigs peeking out from house)* No way, José! It's our lives you'll steal!

Wolf: Why do you keep calling me José?! Get ready to feel my fury! *(huffs and puffs and blows the stick house offstage)*

Pigwaldo: *(shivering)* Not again!

Pigwena: *(shivering)* Oh, my! Let's scram! *(both pigs run offstage)*

Wolf: *(chasing)* Ugh . . . so much running!

Narrator:	The hungry wolf chased Pigwaldo and Pigwena all the way to the house of bricks. *(brick house pops up)*
Wolf:	*(to audience, panting)* Whew! These pigs are giving me a run for my money! But they were foolish to lead me here. Now I'll have three times the bacon for my belly!
Wolf:	*(to house)* Little piggies. Little piggies. Let me in for a meal!
Piggero:	*(all pigs peek from behind house)* No way, José! It's our lives you'll steal.
Wolf:	ARRRG! My name is not José! It's Carl! Now behold my fury! *(huffs and puffs, but the brick house stays still)*
Piggero:	Neener! Neener!
Wolf:	*(panting hard)* What! How can it be? Let's try that again. BEHOLD MY FURY! *(huffs and puffs, but the brick house remains standing)*
Wolf:	Cough . . . sputter . . . gasp!
Pigwaldo:	Hee! Hee! Foiled again!
Pigwena:	You can't get us.
Piggero:	My house of bricks is just too strong for your hot air!
Wolf:	*(still panting, turning to the audience)* I'll . . . show . . . them . . . If I can't blow this house over, I'll just climb down the chimney.
Wolf:	*(climbs house)* Look out below! Here I come! *(ducks down behind house)*

Narrator: As the hungry wolf climbed down the chimney, the sneaky little pigs slipped out the back door.

Pigwena: What are we going to do now?!

Piggero: Don't worry. This house isn't just strong. It's smart too. I can lock all of the doors and windows with my voice.

Piggero: HOUSE: LOCK!

Sound Effect: CLICK! CLICK! CLICK!

Pigwaldo: Clever!

Wolf: *(behind house, house shakes)* Hey, who locked all of the doors. Let me out!

Piggero: No way, CARL! You're under house arrest! Now we're going on vacation. *(all pigs walk offstage)*

Wolf: *(house turns around to show wolf)* Aww, shucks. At least I can still raid the refrigerator and surf the internet while they're gone.

The End

Take the Stage!

Your stage is built. Your puppets and props are made. You even know the script by heart. Now it's time to perform your play. Since this story has four characters, ask a friend to join in the fun. Then use these simple tips to put on a dazzling show!

Create Voices

Just like your voice is different from a friend's voice — your puppets can have their own voices too. Think about each character and experiment with voices that fit them best. For example, maybe Pigwaldo and Piggero have lower, male voices, while Pigwena has a higher female voice. Meanwhile, maybe the wolf has a gravelly voice to match his gruff nature.

Develop Personalities

Give each puppet its own personality. Show the audience what each character is like through the way it acts, moves, and speaks. Here are some ideas for giving your puppets personality:

• Is the wolf out of breath after he chases the pigs? If so, make him hunch over and pant heavily after each chase scene. He can even lie down on stage to catch his breath.

• Make the pigs quickly peek around their houses and then duck back behind them. Doing so shows they're scared the wolf will grab them if they stay out too long.

• Exaggerate the puppets' actions and emotions by moving their heads in different ways. Tilt the pigs' heads when they tease the wolf to make them look silly. Swirl around the wolf's head when he blows down the houses to make his breath look more powerful.

Plan Your Movements

During your play, the puppets need to move around and act out the action. Decide ahead of time what they should do. For instance, when the wolf blows the houses down, which direction and how fast should they fly away? And how should the chase scenes with the pigs and wolf look? Should they simply dash offstage or run back and forth in confusion? The choice is yours!

Practice the Play

When you're done planning, it's time to practice. Rehearse the play several times before performing it in front of a real audience. The more times you practice, the better your show will be.

In no time flat, you'll be a pro at putting on a puppet show!

27

The Show Must Go On!

You've performed *The Three Little Pigs* and the show was a success! Time to put away the puppets, right? No way, José! Now that you know what you're doing, you can really get creative. Try these fun ways to change your play and make it unique:

Make up new dialogue to continue the story. For instance, what happens when the pigs return from vacation and the wolf is still in Piggero's house? Let the adventure continue in unexpected ways.

Reverse the roles of the characters. What would happen if the wolf was building houses and the pigs were knocking them down? How would the poor wolf outsmart the mean, nasty pigs?

Change the building materials for the pig's house into types of candy. Imagine if the pigs built their homes with marshmallows, chocolate bars, and candy canes. What might the wolf do differently to try to destroy them?

Come up with a new ending. What would happen if the wolf knocked down the brick house? Would the pigs still get away? Not every story needs a happy ending. Give your tale an unexpected twist.

Conclusion

You've mastered a sock puppet performance of *The Three Little Pigs*. What comes next? Luckily the world is full of classic stories, fairy tales, myths, and fables. Pick a story you like and make your own puppets. Then put on a sock puppet play that's all your own!

Glossary

audience (AW-dee-uhns)—people who watch or listen to a play, movie, or show

character (KAYR-ik-tuhr)—a person or creature in a story

confident (KON-fi-duhnt)—sure of oneself

dialogue (DYE-uh-lawg)—the words spoken between two or more characters

faux (FOH)—made to look like something else through an artistic effect

imagine (i-MAJ-uhn)—to picture something in your mind

material (muh-TIHR-ee-uhl)—the things or substances from which something is made

performance (pur-FOR-muhnss)—the public presentation of a play, movie, or piece of music

personality (pur-suh-NAL-uh-tee)—all of the qualities or traits that make one person different from others

practical (PRAK-tuh-kuhl)—sensible, or showing good judgement

production (pruh-DUHK-shuhn)—a play or any form of entertainment that is presented to others

prop (PROP)—an item used by an actor or performer during a show

rehearsal (ri-HURSS-uhl)—a practice performance of a script

script (SKRIPT)—the story for a play, movie, or television show

skedaddle (ski-DAD-uhl)—to move quickly or run away from something scary

unique (yoo-NEEK)—one of a kind

Read More

Kandel, Tiger, and Heather Schloss. *The Ultimate Sock Puppet Book: Clever Tips, Tricks, and Techniques for Creating Imaginative Sock Puppets.* Minneapolis: Creative Publishing International, 2014.

Petelinsek, Kathleen. *Making Sock Puppets.* How-to Library. Ann Arbor, Mich.: Cherry Lake Publishing, 2015.

Reynolds, Toby. *Making Puppets.* Mini Artist. New York: Windmill Books, 2016.

Internet Sites

Use FactHound to find Internet sites related to this book.

Visit *www.facthound.com*

Just type in 9781515766834 and go.

Check out projects, games and lots more at
www.capstonekids.com

Maker Space Tips

Download tips and tricks for using this book and others in a library maker space.

Visit *www.capstonepub.com/dabblelabresources*

TITLES IN THIS SET: